FORTNIT
Healing Items and Potions

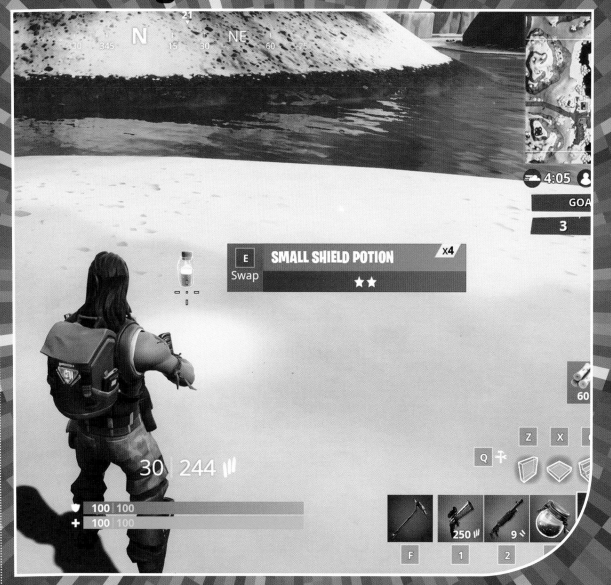

CHERRY LAKE PUBLISHING • ANN ARBOR, MICHIGAN

by Josh Gregory

Published in the United States of America by Cherry Lake Publishing
Ann Arbor, Michigan
www.cherrylakepublishing.com

Reading Adviser: Marla Conn MS, Ed., Literacy specialist, Read-Ability, Inc.

Copyright ©2020 by Cherry Lake Publishing
All rights reserved. No part of this book may be reproduced or utilized in any
form or by any means without written permission from the publisher.

Library of Congress Cataloging-in-Publication Data
Names: Gregory, Josh, author.
Title: Fortnite. Healing items and potions / by Josh Gregory.
Other titles: Healing items and potions
Description: Ann Arbor, Michigan : Cherry Lake Publishing, 2019. | Series:
    Unofficial guides | Series: 21st century skills innovation library |
    Includes bibliographical references and index. | Audience: Grade 4 to 6.
Identifiers: LCCN 2019003336 | ISBN 9781534148161 [lib. bdg.] |
    ISBN 9781534151024 (pbk.) | ISBN 9781534149595 (pdf) |
    ISBN 9781534152458 (ebook)
Subjects: LCSH: Fortnite (Video game)—Juvenile literature.
Classification: LCC G1469.35.F67 G745 2019 | DDC 794.8—dc23
LC record available at https://lccn.loc.gov/2019003336

Cherry Lake Publishing would like to acknowledge the work of the Partnership for
21st Century Learning. Please visit www.p21.org for more information.

Printed in the United States of America
Corporate Graphics

Contents

Chapter 1

Evening the Odds

I f you've played *Fortnite* before, you know just how fun it can be. You get to explore a huge island full of cool locations and exciting gear to pick up. You can build your own forts and towers. You can play with

Piloting a fighter plane is just one of the many, many things you can do in *Fortnite*.

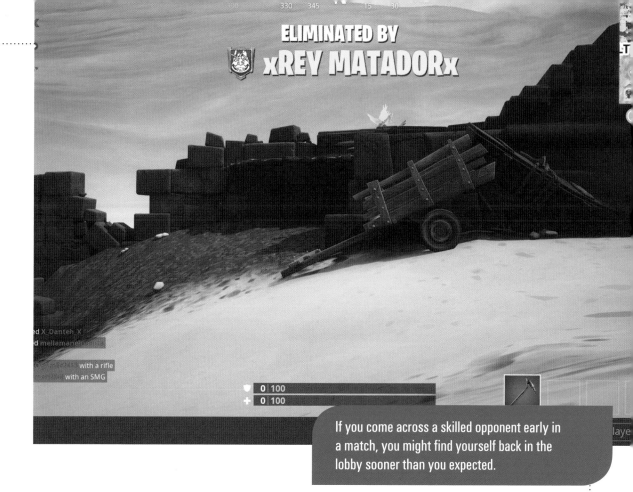

ELIMINATED BY
xREY MATADORx

with a rifle
with an SMG

If you come across a skilled opponent early in a match, you might find yourself back in the lobby sooner than you expected.

your friends and share the game's craziest moments together.

Part of the fun of *Fortnite* is the challenge of battling other players. In each match you play, you'll face off against up to 99 other people. Some of them are likely to be beginners who are just learning how to play. But others could be experienced pros. These players are really good at the game! Taking them on head-to-head could seem almost impossible if you don't have incredible *Fortnite* skills.

Luckily, *Fortnite* is a game with many options. With the right strategies and the right gear, it is

Healing items are some of the most important items you can find in *Fortnite*.

You might need to rely on help from a teammate if you don't use your healing and shield items wisely.

possible for all players to succeed. Even if you don't have perfect aim or lightning-quick reflexes, you can always find a way to get an advantage over your opponents.

One way to give yourself an edge is to take advantage of the many potions and other items you can find scattered around the world of *Fortnite*. Some of these items will help you heal after your character takes

A Lot to Learn

Potions and other items play a big role in *Fortnite*. Learning how to use them correctly is an essential part of becoming a successful player. But while they can give you a big advantage, you simply can't win a match with items alone. You will also need to master the other parts of *Fortnite*. You will have to get good at fighting other players using a variety of different weapons. You will also need to practice your building skills.

As you get better at fighting, building, and other activities in *Fortnite*, you will probably notice that you are also getting better at using items. This is because all of the different parts of *Fortnite* work together. If you are good at building, for example, you will last longer in fights. This will give you more opportunities to use different items.

damage in a fight. Some will charge up your shields. Others will provide you with a wide range of benefits and abilities to help you become the last player standing at the end of the match.

When you first start playing, all of these potions and other items can seem like a lot to keep track of. Which ones will heal you? Which ones are important to hang on to, and which ones are better to

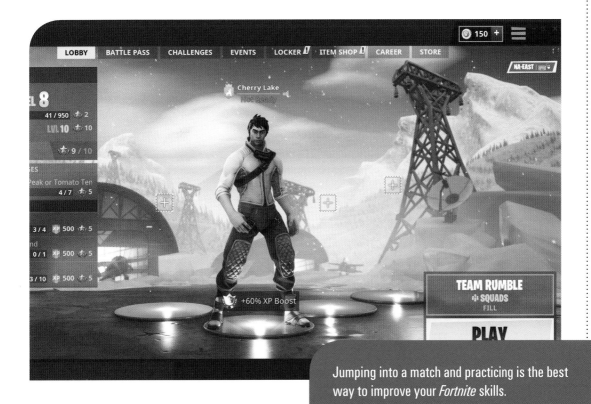

Jumping into a match and practicing is the best way to improve your *Fortnite* skills.

leave behind? Where should you look to find the most useful items? You might figure out the answers to all of these questions by simply playing the game a long time. After all, it can be a lot of fun just to experiment and play around with different items to see how they work. But if you want to quickly go from a beginner to a *Fortnite* pro, it helps to study the game's items ahead of time!

Chapter 2

Health and Shields

One of the most important keys to success in *Fortnite* is keeping your character healthy and well-protected. If you take a bunch of damage during a fight and continue to wander the island while wounded, you can be defeated very quickly by a surprise attack.

Even though this player's health bar is mostly full, she could be defeated quickly because she doesn't have any shields.

You'll start out each match with 100 health and zero shields.

When you start playing *Fortnite*, you will probably notice the two bars near the center-bottom of your screen. The bottom bar is green. It starts out at 100 percent in each match. This bar measures your health.

Your health bar shows how close you are to being defeated. If it reaches zero, you will be knocked out of a match. Your character can take damage in a variety of ways. The most common is to be hit with enemy attacks. Another possible cause of damage is the ever-growing storm that surrounds the playable area of a match. If you get caught in the storm, your character will lose health until you get back into the safety of the storm eye. You can also damage your character through your own mistakes. For example, you will lose health points if you fall from a high place or if you get caught in an explosion from your own grenades or rockets.

The bar above your health bar starts out at zero. As you fill it up, it will turn blue. This bar measures

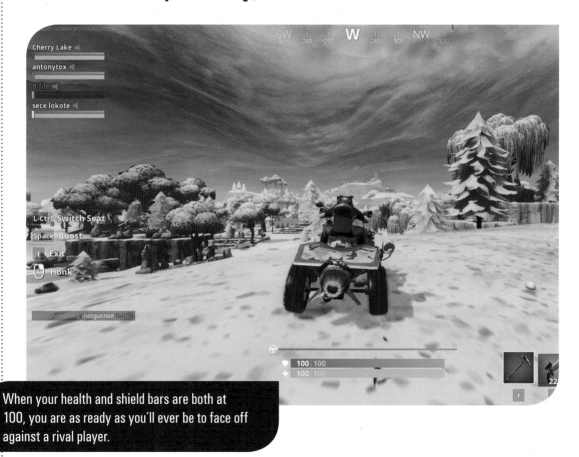

When your health and shield bars are both at 100, you are as ready as you'll ever be to face off against a rival player.

Getting caught in the storm will reduce your health without affecting your shields.

your shields. Your shields will absorb all damage from enemy attacks until the blue bar reaches zero. So for example, if you have 25 shield points, your enemies will have to damage you for 25 points before your health bar will start dropping. Be careful, though. While shields are incredibly important, they don't protect all the time. If you take damage from a fall or from getting caught in the storm, it will skip right past your shields and cause your health bar to start dropping.

One of the most fun ways to play *Fortnite* is to team up with your friends in Duos or Squads. In these

Sharing Is Caring

Teamwork is a key to your success in *Fortnite*'s Duos and Squads. You will not stand much of a chance if you try to take on enemy teams by yourself and ignore your teammates. Instead, you should work together, stay close to your teammates, and avoid getting cornered by an enemy team. Build walls to protect your teammates. Attack enemies from many sides at once. The possibilities for team strategies are nearly endless.

Items can play a big role in your team strategies. Maybe your teammates are low on health, but you have plenty of healing items. Open your **inventory** and drop some items on the ground for your teammates to use. Be sure you are in a safe area, though. Let your teammates know you are going to share some items. You don't want an enemy player to sneak in and grab the things you drop!

modes, health works a little bit differently than it does in Solo mode. When your health reaches zero, you are not automatically eliminated from a match. Instead, your character will be knocked down. You will no longer be able to use weapons or items. You can move around, but your character can only crawl slowly. You will also notice that your health and shield bars have been replaced with a red bar that slowly counts down from 100. When this happens, do your best to get to a location with plenty of cover. You will have about one minute before the bar reaches zero.

Your teammates will be alerted that your character is knocked down. This is their cue to come rescue you. If a teammate reaches you before your red bar reaches zero, they can **revive** you. However, this takes a few seconds, and your teammate will not be able to attack while reviving you. Your character is also very **vulnerable** while knocked down. If an enemy attacks you during this time, your red bar will decrease even faster, and you can be eliminated from the match very quickly.

You should try to keep both your health and shield bars as full as you can at all times. You never know when you will make a mistake or get caught in a surprise attack. Luckily, there are plenty of items you can use to keep your character strong and healthy.

Chapter 3

All Kinds of Items

There are many different items in *Fortnite*, and each one has its own pros and cons. In the middle of a hectic fight, you don't always have time to carefully compare each item's **statistics** before

Opening the inventory screen in the middle of a battle is usually a bad idea, but you can take a look at your items if you are in a safe location.

you pick it up. This means you have to memorize what each one does if you want to make good decisions.

Some of the most crucial items are the ones that can restore your health bar. For example, bandages are common items that you will find all over the island. Bandages come in stacks of five, so you get five of them every time you pick up the bandage item off the ground. You can stack up to 15 of them in each inventory space. This means you could pick up three stacks of bandages without losing more than one space.

While you can carry a lot of them, each bandage is a fairly weak way to restore health. A single bandage restores 15 points to your health bar. But you cannot raise your health bar past 75 using bandages. You will need different items if you want to get it all the way back to 100.

The medkit is another common healing item. It is much stronger than a bandage. Each medkit raises your health bar all the way to 100. You can't carry very many of them. They come in stacks of one, and the maximum stack per inventory space is three. But even one or two medkits is usually better than carrying a ton of bandages.

Another way to restore health is to eat apples. You will find apples sitting on the ground near trees. There are usually a few of them grouped near each other. So if you see one, try looking around for some more. Each apple you eat will raise your health bar by five points. You can raise it all the way to 100 if you find enough apples. Unlike most items, apples do not take up inventory spaces. In fact, you can't carry them with you at all. Your character will eat them as soon as you

Finding an apple on the ground is like finding free health points. Eat every one you can!

Here Today, Gone Tomorrow

Sometimes *Fortnite*'s **developers** will add or remove items from the game. They often do this as a surprise or as part of a larger event in the game. For example, in summer 2018, the game celebrated its first birthday. The developers added birthday cakes all around the island. Each cake had slices placed nearby for players to pick up. The slices worked like apples or mushrooms, but they were even better. They restored five health points and five shield points per piece!

Another limited-time item in *Fortnite* was the jetpack. This fun item let players zoom through the sky. The shadow stone was an item that was available only in fall 2018. When used, it turned players invisible for a short time. However, they could not fire their weapons while invisible.

Items removed from *Fortnite* are said to be "in the vault." But the *Fortnite* developers are always thinking about ways to bring back popular vaulted items. You never know when your favorites might make another appearance in the game!

pick them up. They are always worth grabbing if you find them and your health is less than 100.

The Cozy Campfire is a unique healing item that works a little differently from the others. This item does not take up space in your inventory, and you cannot use it directly. Instead, it is technically a type of trap that you can use when building. After picking up a Cozy Campfire trap, you can place it on the floor of any structure you build. While most traps are harmful, this one can heal you. Stand near the campfire to start healing at a rate of two points per second. The campfire only lasts for 25 seconds, so the most you can get from it is 50 health points. It is especially useful in the Duos or Squads modes. All of your teammates can gather around at the same time to share the healing benefits.

Shield items work much like healing items. The most basic kind is the Small Shield Potion. Each one will raise your shield bar by 25 points. Like bandages, this item has a limit. You cannot raise your shields above 50 with Small Shield Potions. Small Shield Potions come in stacks of three, and you can hold up to 10 of them in a single inventory space.

The next step up from the Small Shield Potion is the regular Shield Potion. Shield Potions drop one at a time, and you can stack up to three of them in an inventory space. Each Shield Potion raises your shield bar by 50 points. Using two of them can raise your shield bar all the way to 100.

Mushrooms are another very useful item. They work exactly like apples, except they raise your

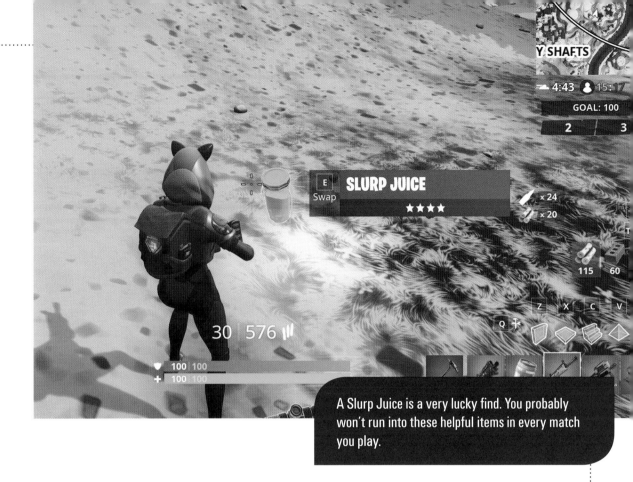

A Slurp Juice is a very lucky find. You probably won't run into these helpful items in every match you play.

shields instead of your health. Like apples, you should stop to pick up mushrooms whenever you can.

If you are lucky in a *Fortnite* match, you will find some of the extremely useful items that can restore both health and shields. One of these items is called Slurp Juice. You will find Slurp Juice one at a time, and you can stack up to two in each inventory space. When you use a Slurp Juice, it will start raising your health bar by one point every 0.5 seconds. It will continue until it has restored 75 points. The best part is that once your health hits 100, the Slurp Juice will start restoring your shields until it has restored its total 75 points. So, for example, let's imagine your health bar is at 75 and your shield bar is at zero. A Slurp Juice would bring you up to 100 health and 50 shields. This is super useful!

Even better than Slurp Juice is the mighty Chug Jug. The Chug Jug is the best healing item in the game. It restores both your health and shield bars to a full 100 percent. The downside is that you can only fit one

Consider yourself lucky any time you find a Chug Jug. This is the jackpot of healing items!

Chug Jug in each inventory space. This means you can't carry very many of them. However, Chug Jugs are fairly hard to find, so you are unlikely to find more than one per match anyway.

In addition to healing and shield items, *Fortnite* is packed with other interesting tools. Try picking up a pack of balloons. You can inflate one, two, or three at a time. With one or two inflated, you will be able to jump higher. You will also fall more slowly, so you won't take damage when dropping from heights. With three inflated, you'll start to slowly float into the air! But watch out—other players can shoot the balloons to make them pop.

You can also pick up an item called the Bush. The Bush is exactly what it sounds like: a green, leafy bush. You can wear it as a disguise. When crouched, you will blend in quite well with the surrounding scenery. Be careful, though. Experienced players know that enemies might disguise themselves, so they keep an eye out and attack suspicious bushes.

Chapter 4

Strategic Thinking

Using any item whenever you feel like it will not get you very far in *Fortnite*. Instead, you'll need to think strategically. Which items should you pick up? Which ones should you drop or leave behind? When should you use your items? These are all things to consider as you play.

While bandages aren't very helpful when your health is already high, you might want to carry them for later if you don't have any other healing items.

You will see a countdown timer above your health and shield bars anytime you drink a potion or use a healing item.

Each healing or shield item in *Fortnite* takes a certain amount of time to use. For example, you will need to stand still for 4 seconds to apply a bandage. It takes a full 15 seconds to use a Chug Jug. During this time, you cannot move or fire your weapons. This means you are very vulnerable to attacks. On top of that, because you are healing, your character is probably already injured in the first place.

What this all means is that you should never try to drink a potion or use a healing item while you are in the line of fire. Try to defeat your enemy before healing, if you can. If you can't wait, find or build yourself some cover before using your item.

If you aren't in the middle of a fight, consider using your healing items as soon as you can. There

It is usually a good idea to throw up a few simple walls before drinking a potion.

Practice Makes Perfect

No matter how much you learn about *Fortnite*, your knowledge is no good unless you can put it into use in real game situations. The only way to do this is to jump in and start playing matches. Chances are high that you'll lose often at first. You might find yourself thinking, "I knew how to do that. I just wasn't fast enough!" Don't worry. The more you practice, the more your skills and reflexes will sharpen. You will be able to put all of your knowledge about the game's items to use, and playing will seem like second nature. Soon enough, you'll find yourself winning more often.

is no advantage to running around with low health or shields. Your items take up valuable space in your inventory. Using them up will help you last longer in the match and give you space to pick up more stuff as you find it. It is often a good idea to use items as soon as you get them.

If you're playing well, your inventory could be full of quality items while your health and shields are maxed out. In this situation, only pick up healing items if they are better than the ones you already have. For example, replace bandages with medkits. Replace Small Shield Potions with regular-size Shield Potions. Replace just about anything with a Chug Jug!

Choosing the right time to drink a Slurp Juice is all part of the strategic thinking you'll need to win in *Fortnite*.

Always use other healing items before drinking Slurp Juice. If your health is maxed out, the Slurp Juice points will all go into your shield. If your health is less than 100, some of the points will be spent on health when they could be going toward shields.

You should never leave a Slurp Juice behind, even if you already have plenty of healing items and your health and shields are high. Just take it and drink it

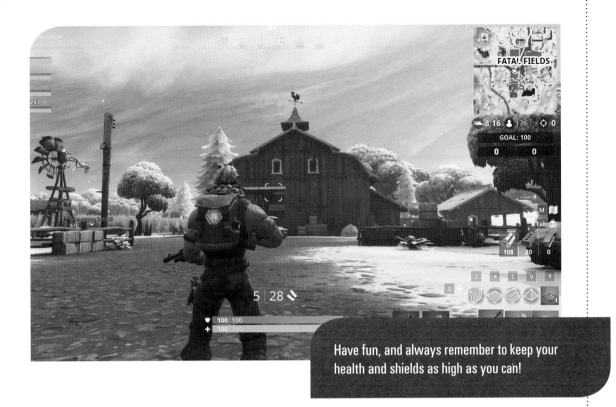

Have fun, and always remember to keep your health and shields as high as you can!

anyway. This will keep rival players from getting to use it!

Once you've mastered potions and other items in *Fortnite*, you'll be well on your way to becoming a pro. You'll stay in matches longer, and you'll be able to pull off crazy tricks against your opponents. Good luck!

Glossary

developers (dih-VEL-uh-purz) people who make video games or other computer programs

inventory (IN-vuhn-toh-ree) a list of the items your character is carrying

revive (rih-VIVE) to bring back to life

statistics (stuh-TIS-tiks) numerical measurements

vulnerable (VUL-nur-uh-buhl) able to be attacked

Find Out More

BOOKS

Cunningham, Kevin. *Video Game Designer*. Ann Arbor, MI:
Cherry Lake Publishing, 2016.

Powell, Marie. *Asking Questions About Video Games*. Ann Arbor,
MI: Cherry Lake Publishing, 2016.

WEBSITES

Epic Games—Fortnite
www.epicgames.com/fortnite/en-US/home
Check out the official *Fortnite* website.

Fortnite Wiki
https://fortnite.gamepedia.com/Fortnite_Wiki
This fan-made website offers up-to-date information on the
latest additions to *Fortnite*.

Index

About the Author

Josh Gregory is the author of more than 125 books for kids. He has written about everything from animals to technology to history. A graduate of the University of Missouri–Columbia, he currently lives in Chicago, Illinois.